W9-BMT-737

EDGE
BOOKS™

PRO SPORTS
by the Numbers

PRO HOCKEY
by the Numbers

by Todd Kortemeier

Consultant:
Roger Godin, Team Curator, Minnesota Wild

CAPSTONE PRESS
a capstone imprint

Edge Books arc published by Capstone Press, 1710 Roe Crest Drive, North Mankato, Minnesota 56003
www.mycapstone.com

Library of Congress Cataloging-in-Publication Data
Names: Kortemeier, Todd, 1986-
Title: Pro hockey by the numbers / by Todd Kortemeier.
Description: North Mankato, Minnesota : An imprint of Capstone Press, [2016]
| Series: Edge Books. Pro Sports by the Numbers | Includes bibliographical
references and index. | Audience: Age: 11. | Audience: Grades: 4 to 6.
Identifiers: LCCN 2015037141| ISBN 9781491490570 (library binding) | ISBN
9781491490617 (paperback) | ISBN 9781491490655 (eBook PDF) | ISBN
9781491490693 (paperback)
Subjects: LCSH: Hockey--Miscellanea--Juvenile literature.
Classification: LCC GV847.25 .K67 2016 | DDC 796.962--dc23
LC record available at http://lccn.loc.gov/2015037141

Editorial Credits
Patrick Donnelly, editor
Nikki Farinella, designer
Jake Nordby, production specialist

Photo Credits
AP Images: Kostas Lymperopoulos/Cal Sport Media, cover (bottom), 1 (foreground), 19 (bottom), Philippe Bouchard/Cal Sport Media, cover (top), 14 (bottom); Getty Images: 13, Bruce Bennett Studios, 22 (trophy), Denis Brodeur/NHLI, 20; Kristina Servant CC2.0, 29; Newscom: David Saffran/ICON SMI 330, 17 (left), Del Mecum/Cal Sport Media, 19 (top), IHA/ICON SMI, 23 (middle left), Jason Szenes/UPI Photo Service, 21, Kostas Lymperopoulos/Cal Sport Media, 25 (top), Mark LoMoglio/Icon Sportswire CCX, 18, STR/Reuters, 16–17, 17 (right); Red Line Editorial, 6, 14 (top), 22 (jerseys), 24 (silhouettes), 26, 27; Samuil_Levich/iStockphoto, 8–9 (foreground); Shutterstock Images: Adam Vilimek, 6–7, Alexander Kaludov, cover (right), 4, 14–15, AlexRoz, 12, 28, Alhovik, 24 (net), 25 (middle), Antony McAulay, 7, bergserg, 4–5, chrupka, 10–11, CLIPAREA I Custom media, 9, exopixel, 25 (bottom), GoodMood Photo, 18–19, itlada, 17 (background), 24–25, K13 ART, 8, mariakraynova, 8–9 (background), Pinkcandy, 28–29, Prixel Creative, 15, 23 (top), sabri deniz kizil, 10, 23 (middle right), 27, 29, Webspark, cover (background), 1 (background), yyang, 23 (bottom), 26–27, 28

Design Elements
Red Line Editorial (infographics), Shutterstock Images (perspective background, player silhouettes)

Printed in the United States of America in Mankato, Minnesota
102015   2015CAP

TABLE OF CONTENTS

THE ORIGINAL SIX

For most of its early history, the National Hockey League (NHL) struggled to keep teams around. But the league reached a period of stability from the 1942–43 season through the 1966–67 season. Six of its oldest teams were the only members of a six-team league for those 25 years. Those teams came to be known as the "Original Six." They are still in the league today. Many other teams have come and gone. Check out the map to trace the roots of the 30 current NHL teams—when they were established, and where many of them began.

EDMONTON OILERS, 1979

CALGARY FLAMES, 1980

VANCOUVER CANUCKS, 1970

SAN JOSE SHARKS, 1991

COLORADO AVALANCHE, 1995
COLORADO ROCKIES, 1976

LOS ANGELES KINGS, 1967
ANAHEIM DUCKS, 1993

ARIZONA COYOTES, 1996

CLASS OF '67

The NHL doubled in size for the 1967–68 season. Six new teams joined the Original Six as the league stretched its footprint from coast to coast. The Class of '67 included:

LOS ANGELES KINGS
MINNESOTA NORTH STARS
  (LATER MOVED TO DALLAS)
OAKLAND SEALS (LATER MOVED
  TO CLEVELAND, THEN MERGED
  WITH THE NORTH STARS)

• PHILADELPHIA FLYERS
• PITTSBURGH PENGUINS
• ST. LOUIS BLUES

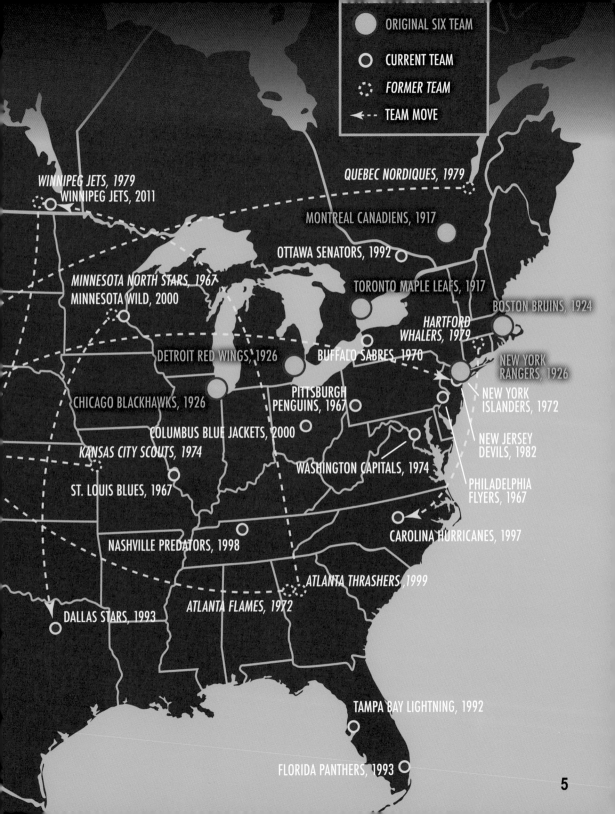

WINNIPEG JETS, 1979
WINNIPEG JETS, 2011

QUEBEC NORDIQUES, 1979

MONTREAL CANADIENS, 1917

OTTAWA SENATORS, 1992

MINNESOTA NORTH STARS, 1967
MINNESOTA WILD, 2000

TORONTO MAPLE LEAFS, 1917

BOSTON BRUINS, 1924

HARTFORD
WHALERS, 1979

DETROIT RED WINGS, 1926

BUFFALO SABRES, 1970

NEW YORK
RANGERS, 1926

PITTSBURGH
PENGUINS, 1967

CHICAGO BLACKHAWKS, 1926

NEW YORK
ISLANDERS, 1972

COLUMBUS BLUE JACKETS, 2000

KANSAS CITY SCOUTS, 1974

NEW JERSEY
DEVILS, 1982

WASHINGTON CAPITALS, 1974

ST. LOUIS BLUES, 1967

PHILADELPHIA
FLYERS, 1967

NASHVILLE PREDATORS, 1998

CAROLINA HURRICANES, 1997

ATLANTA THRASHERS, 1999

DALLAS STARS, 1993

ATLANTA FLAMES, 1972

TAMPA BAY LIGHTNING, 1992

FLORIDA PANTHERS, 1993

ORIGINAL SIX TEAM

CURRENT TEAM

FORMER TEAM

TEAM MOVE

5

THE RINK

An NHL rink is bound on all sides by boards and glass. It must be sturdy to contain the blistering shots, hard hits, and wild action on the ice.

0.75 inches
ice thickness

16 degrees Fahrenheit
ice temperature

Skating Surface

Chilled concrete slab

Insulation

Heated concrete

Coolant pipe

Sand and gravel base

Ground water drain

The Winter Classic

In 2008 the NHL began holding a yearly outdoor game called the Winter Classic. Two teams are chosen to play an outdoor game at a temporary rink built in a baseball or football stadium.

8 number of Winter Classics held as of 2016

105,491 record attendance at the Winter Classic, set at Michigan Stadium in 2014

13 degrees Fahrenheit temperature for the 2014 game, the coldest ever

53 feet length of the refrigeration unit used for outdoor games, the biggest of its kind in the world

3,000 gallons of coolant used to keep the rink frozen in Washington, DC, at the 2015 Winter Classic

243 panels of ice that make up the rink

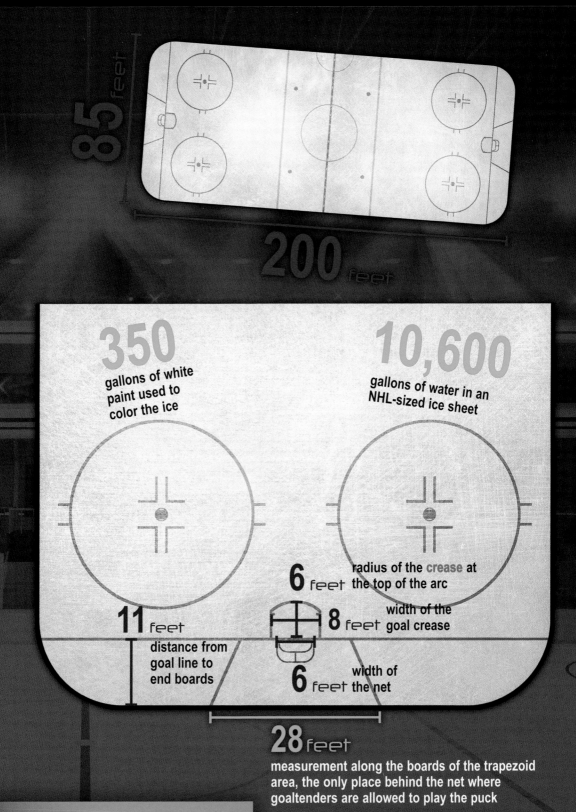

85 feet

200 feet

350
gallons of white paint used to color the ice

10,600
gallons of water in an NHL-sized ice sheet

6 feet radius of the crease at the top of the arc

8 feet width of the goal crease

11 feet distance from goal line to end boards

6 feet width of the net

28 feet
measurement along the boards of the trapezoid area, the only place behind the net where goaltenders are allowed to play the puck

crease: the area where the goalie stands surrounding the net

STICKS, SKATES, AND

Hockey is played with a lot of protective gear, but the game really requires only a basic set of equipment. The items are simple, but technology has played a big role in improving the equipment. It helps players skate faster and shoot harder.

Stick

0.75 inches
maximum curve of blade

63 inches maximum length of shaft

Hockey sticks once were made of wood, but NHL players now rely on models made from composite materials.

12.5 inches
maximum length of blade

Skates

$799
retail price of a pair of Reebok Ribcor Pump hockey skates, worn by Pittsburgh Penguins captain Sidney Crosby

1/8 inch
width of skate blade

3 inches
maximum width of blade

$229.99
price of a Warrior Widow SE stick, a popular NHL model

8

composite: a blend of light but strong materials used to make hockey sticks

PUCKS

72–120 average number of sticks a player uses per season

60,000 approximate number of sticks used in the NHL regular season

Puck

2 minutes
maximum game time a puck is used before it is replaced with a frozen one

5.5–6 ounces
weight of puck

14 degrees Fahrenheit
temperature at which game pucks are stored

80
pucks provided per game

3 inches
diameter of puck

1 inch
thickness of puck

25–30
average number of pucks used in a game

15
pucks brought out for use at the start of each period

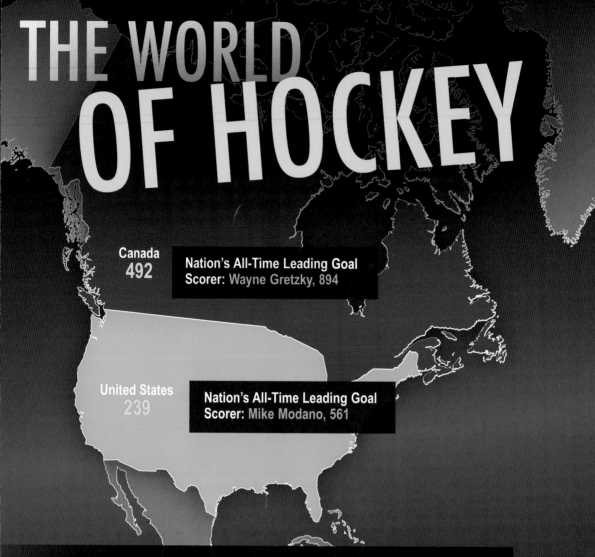

THE WORLD OF HOCKEY

Canada
492

Nation's All-Time Leading Goal
Scorer: Wayne Gretzky, 894

United States
239

Nation's All-Time Leading Goal
Scorer: Mike Modano, 561

Each of the 30 NHL teams has 23 players on its roster. If all players who were on an NHL roster in the 2014–15 season were condensed into one 23-man roster, here is where they would be from.

11.5 players: Canada
5.75 players: United States
1.75 players: Sweden
1 player: Czech Republic
0.75 players: Russia
0.75 players: Finland
0.25 players: Slovakia
0.25 players: Switzerland
0.25 players: Germany
0.75 players: rest of the world

Brazil
1

Canadians developed hockey, but its popularity has spread throughout the world. Players come to the NHL from every corner of the globe, and many countries have high-quality leagues of their own. See where the players who were active in the 2014–15 NHL season came from.

MAP KEY

A. Norway: 1
B. Sweden: 74
C. Finland: 34
D. Estonia: 1
E. Latvia: 1
F. Lithuania: 1
G. Belarus: 1
H. Denmark: 8
I. Germany: 11
J. France: 2
K. Czech Republic: 37
L. Switzerland: 12
M. Austria: 5
N. Slovakia: 12
O. Italy: 1
P. Slovenia: 1

Nation's All-Time Leading Goal Scorer: Teemu Selanne, 684

Nation's All-Time Leading Goal Scorer: Mats Sundin, 564

Nation's All-Time Leading Goal Scorer: Peter Bondra, 503

Nation's All-Time Leading Goal Scorer: Jaromir Jagr, 722

Russia
35

Kazakhstan
2

Brunei
1

11

WHAT'S THE POINT

The NHL standings look a little different from those of other sports. NHL teams have wins and losses, but those results are expressed using points.

2 points — Teams earn 2 points for winning a game in regulation time, in overtime, or in a shootout.

0 points — Teams earn no points for losing in regulation.

1 point — Teams earn 1 point if they lose in overtime or in a shootout.

Atlantic Division		W	L	OTL	PTS
1	Montreal	50	22	10	110
2	Tampa Bay	50	24	8	108
3	Detroit	43	25	14	100
4	Ottawa	43	26	13	99
5	Boston	41	27	14	96
6	Florida	38	29	15	91
7	Toronto	30	44	8	68
8	Buffalo	23	51	8	54

To understand the points system, you first need to know a little about how an NHL game can play out. Every game features 3 periods of 20 minutes. If the score is tied after 60 minutes, a 5-minute overtime period is played with 3 skaters per side. If either team scores, the game is over. If the score is still tied after overtime, there is a shootout. 3 skaters from each team take turns trying to score 1-on-1 against the opposing goalie. The most goals scored wins the game.

TEAMS WITH THE MOST AND FEWEST POINTS SINCE 1974–75

132 Most Points in a Season: 1976–77 Montreal Canadiens

21 Fewest Points in a Season: 1974–75 Washington Capitals

But there's another kind of point in hockey. Players earn points for their play on the ice. Goals and assists are each worth 1 point. These points don't show up in the team standings. But players who pile up goals and assists can help their teams win a lot of games.

DARRYL SITTLER

On February 7, 1976, Toronto Maple Leafs center Darryl Sittler shattered the record for points in a single game. Sittler recorded 6 goals and 4 assists for a total of 10 points in an 11–4 win over the Boston Bruins. Several players are tied for second with 8 points in a game.

WAYNE GRETZKY

Career Leaders in Average Points per Game
1. WAYNE GRETZKY, 1.92
2. MARIO LEMIEUX, 1.88
3. MIKE BOSSY, 1.49

Career Playoff Points Leaders
1. WAYNE GRETZKY, 382
2. MARK MESSIER, 295
3. JARI KURRI, 233

Single-Season Points Leaders
1. WAYNE GRETZKY, 215, 1985–86
2. WAYNE GRETZKY, 212, 1981–82
3. WAYNE GRETZKY, 208, 1984–85

Career NHL Points Leaders
1. WAYNE GRETZKY, 2,857
2. MARK MESSIER, 1,887
3. GORDIE HOWE, 1,850

assist: a pass or a shot that sets up a teammate to score a goal

ON THE POWER PLAY

Committing a penalty doesn't punish only the guilty player. It punishes his team, because he has to sit in the penalty box for a few minutes while his team plays shorthanded.

EXAMPLES OF PENALTIES

a minor penalty (example: **cross-checking, holding, hooking, interference, roughing, tripping**)

a double minor penalty, more severe but not serious enough for a major (example: **high-sticking** or **slashing** that draws blood)

a major penalty (example: fighting)

a misconduct penalty (example: verbal abuse)

EJECTION

a game misconduct penalty (example: a check that results in a head injury)

PERCENTAGE OF MINOR PENALTIES CALLED IN 2014–15

- Hooking
- Tripping
- Roughing
- Holding
- Interference
- Slashing
- High-sticking
- Cross-checking
- Other

PENALTY SHOT

If a player is tripped, hooked, or otherwise illegally denied a clear goal-scoring opportunity, a penalty shot may be awarded. Similar to a shootout, the player tries to score one-on-one against the goalie. In 2014–15, 14 of 41 penalty shots (34.1%) were successful.

cross-checking: shoving an opponent with the stick while holding it with both hands
hooking: using the stick to slow down or turn an opponent

interference: restricting the movement of a player without the puck
high-sticking: hitting an opponent with the stick above the shoulder
slashing: swinging and striking an opponent with the stick

THE FIGHTERS

Fighting is against the rules in hockey, but it still happens. It has become a part of the game to such a degree that players who specialize in fighting are known as "enforcers." It carries with it an automatic penalty of 5 minutes, so it's no surprise that most of the career leaders in penalty minutes were known for fighting.

MOST CAREER PENALTY MINUTES

1. Tiger Williams, 3,966

2. Dale Hunter, 3,565

3. Tie Domi, 3,515

Power Play Effectiveness

Having an extra player on the ice can be a huge advantage. Teams that score consistently on the power play usually end up winning. The reverse is also true. Shutting down the opponent while you're playing shorthanded—also known as killing a penalty—can make a big difference.

BEST POWER PLAY EVER

The 1977–78 Montreal Canadiens scored on 31.9% of their power plays. The NHL average that year was 21.4%.

BEST PENALTY KILL EVER

The 2011–12 New Jersey Devils killed 89.6% of the power plays they faced. The NHL average that year was 82.7%.

POWER PLAY

SHORTHANDED GOALS

One of the best ways to ruin an opponent's power play is by scoring a goal. These players are the career leaders in shorthanded goals.

1. Wayne Gretzky **73**

2. Mark Messier **63**

3. Steve Yzerman **50**

THE STANLEY CUP

The Stanley Cup is one of the most famous trophies in sports. Lifting it in the air after winning the Stanley Cup Final would be the highlight of any player's career. Here are some facts about Lord Stanley's cup.

How it got its name

Sir Frederick Arthur Stanley, a Canadian politician, donated the cup in 1892. It was originally a challenge trophy and then later awarded to the champions of three different leagues. Since 1926 it's been the reward for winning the NHL championship.

1893
year first awarded

1907
first team names engraved on the cup

1919
cup not awarded due to influenza outbreak

35 inches

7.5
inches

34.5
pounds
weight of the cup

24
most cups won
(Montreal Canadiens)

2,476
names on the cup
through 2015

11
most appearances on
the cup (Henri Richard)

12
number of women whose
names are on the cup,
including Marguerite Norris,
President of the Detroit Red
Wings in 1954 and 1955, and
several members of the Ilitch
family, who own the Red Wings

35.25
inches

24

Each player from the winning team gets 24 hours with the cup. Some of the things the cup has seen and done:

Oilers forward Mark Messier celebrated a bit too recklessly and dented the cup. Messier took it to an auto body shop to get it repaired.

Colorado Avalanche defenseman Sylvain Lefebvre had his child baptized in the bowl of the cup.

Red Wings center Steve Yzerman wouldn't let the cup out of his sight. He even showered with it.

Tomas Kopecky (left) of the Detroit Red Wings ate soup out of the cup in his home country of Slovakia.

17.25 inches

2

number of spots available on lowest ring after 2015, meaning a ring will have to be replaced after 2016–17. Once a ring fills up, each ring shifts up a level on the cup. The oldest ring is sent to the Hockey Hall of Fame in Toronto, Canada. Currently, the oldest ring on the cup lists winners from 1954 through 1965.

52

number of names allowed per winning team

13

number of teams each ring can hold

New York Rangers 1993–94

17

THE NETMINDER

It takes a lot of guts to stand in front of an NHL net. Goalies face hard discs of rubber flying at them at more than 100 miles per hour every game.

Target Practice

In the 2014–15 season Chicago Blackhawks goalie Corey Crawford gave up 126 goals. Where was a shooter's best chance to beat him? Check out the graphic to see where Crawford was most vulnerable.

So if players want to beat Crawford, their best bet is to shoot high over his left shoulder. That is called his "glove side." If players are shooting lower, they should aim to his right—also called his "stick side."

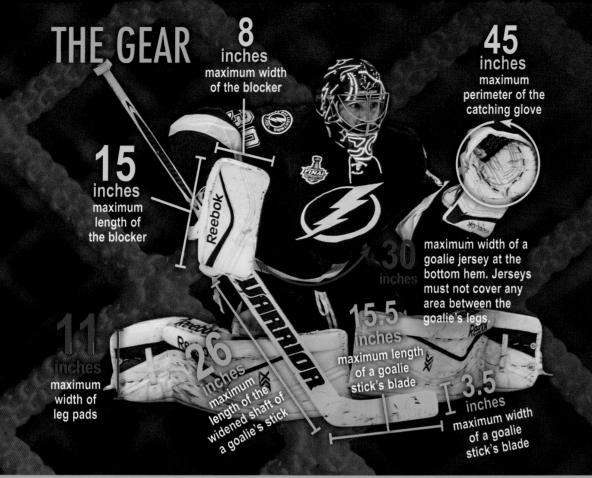

THE GEAR

8 inches
maximum width of the blocker

45 inches
maximum perimeter of the catching glove

15 inches
maximum length of the blocker

maximum width of a goalie jersey at the bottom hem. Jerseys must not cover any area between the goalie's legs.

30 inches

11 inches
maximum width of leg pads

26 inches
maximum length of the widened shaft of a goalie's stick

15.5 inches
maximum length of a goalie stick's blade

3.5 inches
maximum width of a goalie stick's blade

Goalies are evaluated on two main statistics. Goals-against average measures how many goals a goalie gives up per game. An average of 3.00 means the goalie gives up three goals in a typical game. But a goalie who plays for a team with a strong defense doesn't face as many shots as other goalies. That's where save percentage is useful. It compares the number of shots a goalie stops to the number of goals he allows. A goalie with a save percentage of .900 stops 90 percent—or 9 out of 10—of the shots he faces.

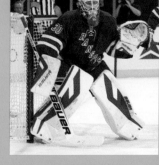

CAREER LEADERS IN GOALS-AGAINST AVERAGE

1. ALEC CONNELL (1924–37), 1.91
2. GEORGE HAINSWORTH (1926–37), 1.93
3. CHARLIE GARDINER (1927–34), 2.02

CAREER LEADERS IN SAVE PERCENTAGE

1. TUUKKA RASK (2007–), .926
2. DOMINIK HASEK (1990–2008), .922
3. HENRIK LUNDQVIST (2005–), .921

blocker: a glove goalies wear with a wide pad on the back to deflect shots

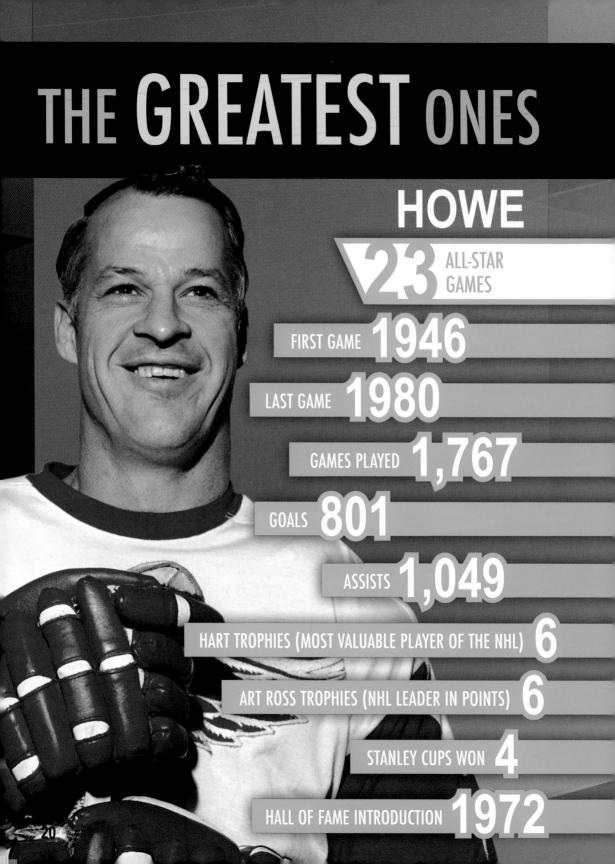

THE GREATEST ONES

HOWE

23 ALL-STAR GAMES

FIRST GAME	**1946**
LAST GAME	**1980**
GAMES PLAYED	**1,767**
GOALS	**801**
ASSISTS	**1,049**
HART TROPHIES (MOST VALUABLE PLAYER OF THE NHL)	**6**
ART ROSS TROPHIES (NHL LEADER IN POINTS)	**6**
STANLEY CUPS WON	**4**
HALL OF FAME INTRODUCTION	**1972**

Look at any NHL record book and two names will come up again and again: Gordie Howe and Wayne Gretzky. But which player was truly the greatest ever? Compare the numbers and judge for yourself.

GRETZKY

ALL-STAR GAMES	18
FIRST GAME	1979
LAST GAME	1999
GAMES PLAYED	1,487
GOALS	894
ASSISTS	1,963
HART TROPHIES	9
ART ROSS TROPHIES	10
STANLEY CUPS WON	4
HALL OF FAME INTRODUCTION	1999

HOCKEY 9
BY THE 9 S

GREAT PLAYERS TO WEAR

GORDIE HOWE

9

BOBBY HULL

9

MIKE MODANO

9

MAURICE RICHARD

9

9

most Hart Trophies won,
by Wayne Gretzky

WAYNE GRETZKY
worn to honor
Gordie Howe

99

9

faceoff dots on the ice

139 most points by a defenseman in one season, Bobby Orr in 1970–71

9 most 50-goal seasons, Wayne Gretzky and Mike Bossy

9 most goals scored in a Stanley Cup Final, Babe Dye in 1922

9 Stanley Cups won by Scotty Bowman, the most cup wins by a coach

faceoff: two players fight for possession of the puck after it is dropped between them by the referee; used to restart play

23

HOCKEY PLAYER
HIGHS AND LOWS

Hockey players come in all shapes and sizes—and with different abilities. Some are known for their speed, some have a wicked **slapshot**, and some do everything well.

6 feet 9 inches

height of Zdeno Chara (1997–), the tallest player in NHL history

Chara is allowed to play with a stick two inches longer than the maximum, due to his height.

5 feet 3 inches

height of Roy "Shrimp" Worters (1925–1937), the shortest player in NHL history

A Hall of Fame goalie, Worters was barely a foot taller than the top of the goal.

4 feet

height of the goal

slapshot: a hard and fast shot with a long backswing and powerful follow-through

23.0
miles per hour
top speed of Carl Hagelin (2011–), who won the fastest skater competition at the 2012 NHL All-Star Weekend

108.8
miles per hour
the fastest recorded slapshot, by Zdeno Chara in 2012

7
number of teeth lost by Chicago Blackhawks defenseman Duncan Keith (2005–) in Game 4 of the Western Conference Finals in 2010

UP IN THE RAFTERS

One of the highest tributes a team can pay a player is to take his number out of service. This tradition is reserved only for the best of the best. Other players have their numbers honored. Like retired numbers, honored numbers are hung from the ceiling of the team's arena to remind fans of the great players who wore them.

6 players to have their number retired by multiple teams

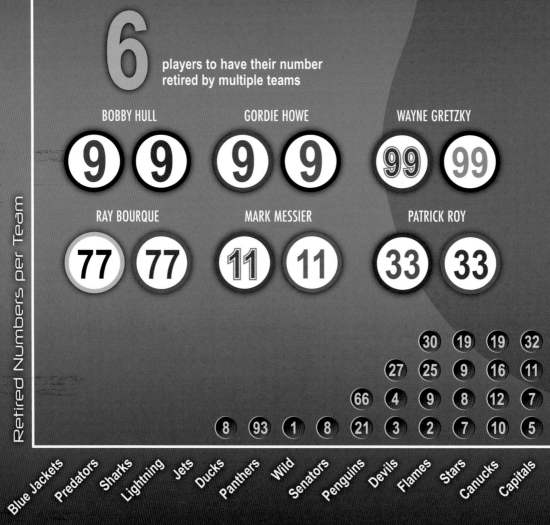

BOBBY HULL	GORDIE HOWE	WAYNE GRETZKY
9 9	9 9	99 99

RAY BOURQUE	MARK MESSIER	PATRICK ROY
77 77	11 11	33 33

Retired Numbers per Team

	30	19	19	32
	27	25	9	16	11
	66	4	9	8	12	7
8	93	1	8	21	3	2	7	10	5

Blue Jackets — Predators — Sharks — Lightning — Jets — Ducks — Panthers — Wild — Senators — Penguins — Devils — Flames — Stars — Canucks — Capitals

SPECIAL CASES

Not every retired or honored number represents a former player.

Wild – No. 1 honors the team's fans.

Panthers – No. 93 honors former team president and general manager Bill Torrey.

retired throughout all of hockey for Wayne Gretzky

Hurricanes	Flyers	Coyotes	Blackhawks	Kings	Islanders	Sabres	Red Wings	Oilers	Rangers	Avalanche	Blues	Bruins	Maple Leafs	Canadiens
														33
														29
														23
												93		19
												27		18
											77		21	16
								77	24	24		17		12
								52	16	15		13		10
			39	19	99	35	33	14	9		10			9
	97	35	99	31	18	12	31	11	26	11	8	9		7
19	16	27	21	30	23	16	10	17	9	21	8	7	7	5
17	7	25	18	20	22	14	9	11	7	19	7	5	6	4
10	4	10	9	18	19	11	7	9	3	16	5	4	5	3
9	2	9	3	16	9	7	5	7	2	8	3	3	4	2
2	1	7	1	4	5	2	1	3	1	3	2	2	1	1

THE DYNASTY

As the Montreal Canadiens approach their 100th NHL season, the franchise clearly stands above all other NHL teams. There are few categories in which the Canadiens don't come out on top. Here are some of the biggest numbers behind the NHL's most successful team.

3,260 most all-time wins

7,476 most all-time points

9

Art Ross Trophy (leading points scorer) winners

24 Stanley Cup wins

12

Norris Trophy (best defenseman) winners

54 Hall of Famers

17 Hart Trophy (NHL most valuable player) winners

29 Vezina Trophy (best goalie) winners

Current goaltender Carey Price won the Hart and Vezina Trophies in 2014–15. Price led the league with a .933 save percentage and 1.96 goals-against average.

Glossary

assist (uh-SISST)—a pass or a shot that sets up a teammate to score a goal

blocker (BLOK-ur)—a glove goalies wear with a wide pad on the back to deflect shots

composite (kuhm-POZ-it)—a blend of light but strong materials used to make hockey sticks

crease (KREESS)—the area where the goalie stands surrounding the net

cross-checking (KRAWSS-CHEK-ing)—shoving an opponent with the stick while holding it with both hands

faceoff (FAYSS-awf)—two players fight for possession of the puck after it is dropped between them by the referee; used to restart play

high-sticking (HYE-STIK-ing)—hitting an opponent with the stick above the shoulder

hooking (HUK-ing)—using the stick to slow down or turn an opponent

interference (in-tur-FIHR-uhnss)—restricting the movement of a player without the puck

slapshot (SLAP-shot)—a hard and fast shot with a long backswing and powerful follow-through

slashing (SLASH-ing)—swinging and striking an opponent with the stick